A Stay in a Sanatorium

A Stay in a Sanatorium
&
other poems

Zbyněk Hejda

translated from the Czech by
Bernard O'Donoghue

from versions by Šimon Daníček

First published in 2005
by Southword Editions,
the Munster Literature Centre,
Frank O'Connor House, 84 Douglas Street,
Cork, Ireland.

Set in Garamond
Printed in Ireland by Colour Books, Dublin.

ISBN: 1-905002-05-X
www.munsterlit.ie

This book is the third in a series of thirteen published
as part of the official programme for Cork 2005
European Capital of Culture

Cover Image: Viki Shock 'A First Size Star' 28 x 35 cm
cartoon collage

Cork 2005
European Capital of Culture

RTÉ   PREMIER
        PARTNER

Grant Aided by
Cork City Council

Comhairle Cathrach Chorcaí

the **arts**
council
an chomhairle
ealaíon

Contents

In the Summer, Now it's Evening

In the summer, now it's evening,
take refuge in the graveyard.
Overhead the birds settling;
below them lines and shadows
where white walls hold the sunlight.
In the paths between the headstones
women with water-jars
from wellside to graveside, back and forth.
Church-door wide open.
Shafts of mote-dust
in the silent space.

But there's one woman praying
in a bench that dwarfs her.
From the chapel garden comes
the sound of laughing: of girls surely.
One hangs out clothes, off-white
from long years of washing.

On tombs along the church wall
inscriptions worn off
by time's working and the weather.

The lime tree's balm falls
on the statue of St John
bent double by its years,
and blackened by the ages.

From the pub across the road
a man reels out. Behind him also
working-girls' voices. You smell burning
from their hard waist-embraces.

The sun goes down
slowly. The shadows grow still longer.

The Evening's Breeze is Mild

Evening breeze is mild.
Late light on the whitewashed wall.
Olive-groves give shading to the twilight,
colours soften to brown or dark gold-green.
The master is here already, with his followers
in the garden's shade. Night comes.
Birds fall silent. The lights go out.
Night-sky deepens; sleep comes
at the end of this long day.

The wind gives a sudden shake
to the leaf-cover on the trees.
The sky plunges downwards.
Trees loom from the darkness.
The thorn hardens in the next wound.

Loneliness drops from the air.
Silence as punishment.
It's no good darkness shrouding the voice.
Everything is asleep.
The bell twists the heart's pain.
Nowhere, no-one, dear God.

In Grandfather's farmyard

In grandfather's farmyard. Music perches on the branches of the majestic chestnut tree. Musicians too have their instruments at the ready, about to start a song, but it's not yet quite time; the music still perches in the trees. The musicians, one after another, climb to the treetop to reach the music. In the process one of them damages his huge Saxhorn. It turns out that part of the instrument is missing; strangely, I am holding the missing part in my hands. I throw it up to him in the branches but it falls back down; it is battered by the branches and lands on the ground, dented. But it is made of soft, pliable metal, so I repair it easily and throw it back up into the branches. The musician catches it and fits it back between the other two parts of the instrument. But the music still doesn't start. We are waiting for something. This makes me anxious, and so does something else – everything is a bit different here. In reality the majestic chestnut tree stands more in the background, as far back as the shed, and there is no chestnut tree at that spot any more. The stump of another chestnut (or of the same one?) is now in the place where really the little wooden summerhouse should be, and so on. Then I get the idea; I am afraid that we are waiting for the start of a funeral.... but, to set against those fears, there is that ease and relaxation in the attitudes of the musicians....

And All Around It Is Full of Music

Knives were drawn across the throats of beasts.
So much music! Yet not one voice!
Again and again a voice said 'God!'
And a bird screamed as if hanging by a hair.

So everywhere around it's full of music
As from dead angels, as from anywhere.
As when music first breaks from the womb,
Or when they start to tune up in the pub.

A Dream

I am walking with someone across the courtyard of a vast complex of buildings, and I am saying to them: 'I live on the boundary of the outside and the inside.' I recognize immediately that this is not quite right and I start correcting myself: 'Before that I lived on the boundary of the inside', by which I suppose I am referring to our shared experience. I had, after all, an apartment with windows onto a narrow road, in the house at the very end. The houses opposite were therefore already outside. It was lonely in that apartment. Now I am living in an equally lonely place, but at least it is inside. Everything is new to me, the old apartment as well as the new one. It is so new that only at this moment am I getting familiar with it all for the first time – both with things far in the past and with the apartment that I used to live in.

And then I am on a train with Jarmila. (How I came so suddenly to be on a train with Jarmila the dream did not explain. It is not even certain that it was later.) We are sitting next to each other in one compartment of an old carriage with wooden benches. Jarmila's distinctive eyes are made up with black shadow. She is sprawling luxuriously on the seat and saying: 'My husband approves of my relationship with you. He understands that it can be of benefit to me…' This has enraged me. I am furious. Jarmila is no longer on the train, she is outside the window and her face is completely different; it is not self-assured any more, but is a helpless, lost face. I was looking at her as if I was only now getting to know her. Tenderness and pity were overwhelming me; when I woke up I was crying.

The Door Will Open

The door will open. Will the dead one enter?
Things will shake gently in the wind.
Yes, she is coming quietly.
It is early spring twilight, and it is raining.

I can hear it still.
It is quieter, and quieter again.

The day was beautiful.
and I yearned for you. But now
in the dark the wind is rising.

In the dark your fingers' touch is fading,
just as the evening sun fades
from college walls in Oxford.

Steps dying away. The dark
and empty chapel.

When we began it was five o'clock,
spring's translucence on the skyline.
Already the twilight was falling
down on the town
with a full white moon.
A shard of music sounding faintly...
will the heart too grow quiet?

The path is narrower, and narrower again.

Behind the path it is still light
as in the depths of the woods
the edge is sensed.

On high
beautiful angels are carrying
the blue canopy of the world
in old pictures
in dark galleries.

Down here
there is unbearable anxiety.

Now the dark is torn
by a bird's cry.

The Man with a Dead Bird

He is growing on the skyline
as he walks…
Then he bends over us,
looks into our dog-faithful eyes
and our skulls crushed underfoot;
then goes on his way.
On our last legs,
we turn our heads
after his retreating back.
It is the man who rose on the skyline
but will not descend in the west.

In the pubs the silence of noon.
Flies on the tables.
Flies in the bottoms of glasses.
Someone passes by,
clearing his throat as he walks.
'It is summer', he says to himself,
and flies migrate through his head.
Meanwhile the birds kill themselves
against the windows. The bartender
takes a bird by its wing…
The throat-clearer says
'It is hot.' 'It is.'
'And what about the bird?'
'Ah, the bird.
If it were not for the flies.'
'And there's no hope of a little rain?'
'It is hot.' 'It is,
and there's no hope…'
The man with a bird

walked barefoot as he was.
And the throat-clearer
observed him at length,
that man with a bird's wing in his hand.

And then at night
the man with the dead bird in his hand
goes round the village.
In the pub someone
is weeping over his glass,
and someone else prefers
to suffocate than cry.
Beneath the tables the legs
of women and men seek each other out.
And over all this sordidness
someone lights a candle.
The village cripple
takes a sip from each one's glass.
The door opens.
'Evening! Evening!'
The man with the bird wing comes
right up to the counter.
It is all falling apart.
Finally they all squash down
in twos.
The dark crackling
of wood is audible.
The man tiptoes lightly
out the door.

They are waiting outside the village with a sidecar
for the man with the bird-wing in his hand.
There is dust on the roads
and off the roads too.
Dust burns around our mouths
as we fight for breath;
already the sap of dust
flows through our innards.
We are gasping silently
for a breath of air,
crouched in the sidecar,
crouchers that we are.
The man is not coming. Somewhere before
the bend in the road he stopped.
He is in no hurry,
carrying from village to village
the case against us: our reeking of drink,
the summer arsons
in which our souls' leaves wither.
When he comes back into view
around the bend,
a dog trails behind him.
A graveyard dog that,
tired already, jumps up in vain
for the hand held high,
carrying by its wing the dead bird.

And the night
when he visited the expectant mother
the bridesmaids all in white strolled
as if it was a Sunday village square.
At all those violated village girls
dogs now held silent.

The fetid moon
glowed as if mouldering
on our sleeping faces.
And of those who were not asleep
he fingered the white breast-skin,
like the crushed leaves
of petalled roses.
It rustled all night.
When he had finished,
the man with the bird wing in his hand,
he went his way again
by road or not by road.
Behind him everywhere
was strewn with offspring.

It's already dark amid the leaves.
After the bout of drizzle
a tree hissed.
As for us,
left to our epidemics,
we were scattering round us —
oh, what were we scattering?
And there were dances in the villages
and chorales played to us by deathly bands
about our blood and sins.
And he,
the man with the dead bird enters,
or enters from the village square.
He has come to drop a feather of the bird.
So then
he started a conversation,
about how it's going to rain
though there's no sign of it.

The wind will not stir:
only music blows through the world
from opening thighs.
Oh there will be village dances
and chorales played for us
about our blood and sins.
And I went,
suffocating in my throat,
weeping, asking what I must confess.

In the Pub Many Voices

In the pub many voices.
I alone; waiting
for the woman who is leaving.
Smoke rises like a prophecy,
then curls beneath the ceiling.
The odd drinker drifts out to the gents.
Darkness and cold get in,
drunks' voices, women's cursing and weeping.
A dog is growling idly, his butcher
already behind the door,
reeking of hides, blood.
Predators too, the whores
are nudging up skirts;
the snakes are hatching.

Death, hardly audible,
no more than a rustle.
Raining outside; amid the leaves
the night-bird's cry is dying.
Despair plunges down on us:
our anxieties like knives.

Glance towards the door: pointless.
Pointless: nobody anywhere.
Everywhere all is sleeping.
Alone, like an assassin.

The Spring Will be Over

The spring will be over.
Also nights when you can't breathe.
As if piled on to a cart
we are lurching towards love-making.

I am full of cheerfulness;
I find everything absurd.
I am full of cheerfulness,
kneeling by a lovely womb.

And it is opening like a flower.
I am sinking into the bowels.
That old joke, that old joke:
it's a grave.

A Shadow is Cast

A shadow is cast.
A whore, still lovely,
is quietly spinning an imperfect garment
with her long fingers.
They made friends roughly.
O love, my love.
Eyes fading, running,
full of flies.
A dead man over a pit.
Music falls from above.
A bride with mint between her thighs
for healing.
In the trees
a leaf will not move.
Those gleams!
And in the pubs life awakens.

The Dream Had a Serene Flow

The dream had a quiet, serene flow to it, a quiet, serene air. We were standing (in Horní Ves) in the main room in front of a small cupboard and everyone was there, including Grandfather who was the centre of that air because I was aware of him the most. All the others were the rest of them, but I don't know which of the rest of them were there. My dear mother was not there. I was explaining to Alena some custom which she hadn't understood, but there was no anxiety from fear that there might be some misunderstanding. This was the issue: a huge salami was to be put where mice could not get at it. Although I saw the whole event extremely vividly – how we are wrapping the salami in paper, the open cupboard: the discussion too was very animated and memorable – all this was of no importance in the dream. As if the meaning was in what wasn't happening now but had been the case before, and this previous state of affairs was all those who were there, particularly Grandfather who has been dead for so many years (an entire eternity). I was aware of Alena's presence as well, but nothing was either astonishing or even surprising to me, it was all so quiet and serene and as if meaningless.

It was the past that had separated itself from me and was indifferently drifting away. The anguish was past.

(Horní Ves: the village in the country where Hejda was born and where he still goes on holiday.Šimon Daníček)

Variations on Macha II

It is so long ago.
It is at the end of the journey.

A long futile wandering,
at the end of which is water.

Thirst, that persevering thirst,
the image of far-away towns,

white, lime-burned.
Sea is *mare*, it is vanishing

from the horizon like
Saint Patrick's ship.

(Macha was the most famous Czech romantic poet who died
young. He travelled to Rome on foot, and composed a famous
erotic diary. S.D.)

Sunsets So Mild

Sunsets so mild.
A grim night is fast approaching.
Screeching of terrified birds.

My dear, my darling, your
hot lips, your lap.

But your face too is already waning.
And what will remain?
Still heartache,
and then?
Love is dying. With a wing
death first brushes,
blazing images are quenched.
They still visit
with light, with scent
on occasion.
But the days are commoner
when the emptiness behind you brightens.

Roads appear again,
gentle inclines, the horizon pure again.
Audible too will be
the moan of hot desire.

Confused from such long suffering,
relieved I tell everyone I meet
that I'm doing fine.

My dear, my darling,
how far from here the sea!

The Japanese Man Has Come Back

The Japanese man has come back after all. But before he came back, she, after stepping slightly aside, says to me apologetically: 'It is not school'. I am trying to understand this: does it mean she is apologising for her lack of schooling in love, that it perhaps wasn't completely perfect? How else can it be understood? It is obvious that we are not in school. Only now the Japanese appears and she says to him at once she is happy, she wants to kiss him. I am finding it rather indecorous, watching her wet lips. She happily tells him what has just happened. He is terrified. He asks with dread: 'And is there going to be a makha?' which means a wedding cake and even a wedding. She says yes of course. The Japanese starts to cry, they are kissing. I feel tears on my cheeks too, only I am not sure whether they are my tears. When the Japanese man is passing near by me I see sorrow and hatred on his face, and my only explanation for his not leaping on me is that he thinks I am crying as well. They are leaving; the Japanese woman has a happy face. She is, it seems, always sincerely happy. She comes back, once more, alone; she is smiling, kissing me affectionately with great tenderness, and she leaves again. Now I know at once that it will always be like that, that she will keep coming back and leaving.

On a Path Dark and Narrow

On a path dark and narrow...
While to the South the sun is sinking,
the early evening lights up briefly
a sliver of landscape shadowed by clouds.

Then a hand will touch me,
sleep's plaster cracking,
a hand so light and smooth in its weaving.
It is morning. The birds are singing.

A Dream of Silence in a Volcano

It was a long and complicated dream. Still vivid in the morning, now, as I am writing it down (13.45), only ruins.

Possibly somewhere in the building of the Faculty of arts or somewhere else where there are lecture rooms, but it was certainly on an embankment. We were in a room that didn't look at all like a lecture room, but it was in a lecture room. There were three of us there: me, Bob, and some other man. Bob was speaking in English but I understood him. I was speaking in Czech but Bob understood me too, although he doesn't speak Czech. No 'but' or 'although'; it was all quite natural and we understood each other. I was asking what he did. Music? Experimental music? That satisfied me: I had expected something like that. What else could he do but experimental music? There was some link there to the words (of some song?) that I attributed to him, but they didn't sound experimental at all, they were beautiful. If it were possible to translate them into Czech – because it was an English song – they would be 'D. is my home.' This was repeated three times, the verb was left out once. The name of the place – I have forgotten it – sounded very English; it began with D.

The song (was it a song?), especially the words and atmosphere – all that was miraculously beautiful. I quickly adapted it: 'Horní Ves is my home.' That was ridiculous. Already at that moment I felt that some catastrophe was coming. Immediately afterwards it became clear that I had misunderstood Bob. He doesn't do experimental music. What do you do then? Silence in a volcano. At that moment a change took place: it had been announcing itself through my anxiety and an uncertain anticipation of what happened next.

I said I had to go. The third man didn't understand anything. He kept asking me why I was leaving, but I gave no explanation. I was leaving defeated, shattered. So Bob does silence in a volcano, maybe a living volcano: was it Etna? Now I understood why Jarmila had to choose Bob. Bob was the greatest. In appearance he was the same Bob I had known before, but in demeanour (and also in importance?) he was someone else entirely: he was an unquestionable leader. And so much was he the greatest that he didn't even display his superiority.

Then in the dream there was also a journey along the embankment from Café Slavia to the faculty. Finally a room, plaster falling off, it was like at home in Hradec. The plaster kept smudging with every least touch of the hand and sliding off the walls: depressing.

from
A Stay in a Sanatorium

A Poem
For my heart,
for my heart,
shall we already end it?

At first the sky was pink in the west,
then lightning chopped the dark thrones of Heaven
and we hid under a tree by a garden wall
somewhere in England
(that dark red building: surely it stands
by the banks of the Thames?),
and then it poured and, as when angels are in ecstasy,
the light of evening trembled and faded upwards.
In the street of St Apolinar
(the gas lamps already lighting)
there appeared a huge red umbrella,
protecting from the rain a couple
staggering beneath its weight.
'Fuck this, can you explain
what kind of umbrella you've brought?
That's no umbrella, it's a parachute.'
And that gentle couple under their parasol
disappeared into the sunny night (strange!),
and it still rained, and the light drizzled softly
at eight o'clock in the evening in early June.

You are still within reach of a hand,
lying quietly on your stomach.
(That was a dream, somewhere in England,
a dream-skeleton, crouched in the mouth of desire.)
I can still feel you in my fingertips,
the thorn of your breast.

Your scent like a night ripped by rain
and lightning.
Why aren't you crying?
What is so funny?
Is it really that funny?
Or is there vast boredom everywhere,
infinite indifference?

The pianist in the café
is drinking like a fish.
That music!
And conversations as if poured

A Stay in a Sanatorium

I was staying at the villa Albertinum
after a Viennese Professor Albert
There were four of us in the room
Mr Rohlena used to say
that his speech is rather slow
since that accidental Once
when he was stacking straw in the loft
snow was lying everywhere
he woke up in the hospital
and as he is waking up
first thing he sees
in the window
the cherry trees in full bloom
Mr Franc was a butcher
his illness was diagnosed
as a stupid
lung cancer
and metastases
whole nights he spent walking
to the toilet from the toilet
from the bathroom to the bathroom
when he wouldn't be back for ages
Mr Rohlena would get up quietly
and sneak out to look for him
Someone said to him
you don't get any sleep Mr Rohlena
But I am worried
he might trap himself somewhere
My third companion was a German from Lanskroun
I've forgotten his name
you didn't see him in the room much
he was hoping, the idiot, he didn't have TB
I don't have what you have, he'd say

and to avoid infection
before going to bed
he'd put a handkerchief over his gob
he spoke little
because speaking makes you breathless
you have to breathe deeply then
and so breathe in more germs
once he did get himself talking
he'd served at the Russian front
we were polishing off
the seriously wounded
what would you expect? he's lost his legs
and maybe his hands as well
plus he was possibly blind
they'd end up saddled with him
his parents or his unfortunate wife
stuck with him the rest of their lives
The revulsion this aroused
quite surprised him
It was humane
we gave them injections
In another villa there lived
a priest from Černilov
I'd have liked to have the odd word with him
but either he wasn't interested
in what I was interested in
or he didn't trust me
He liked talking to old farts and fogeys
about fishing and planting trees
where to put dung and what bait for what fish
it seemed he knew what he was talking about
the old fogeys listened to him
I wrote to Vladimír Holan
and he wrote back
a stimulating letter

Honza Lopatka sent me braces
(you couldn't get braces anywhere)
and a letter that cheered me up
but which I've mislaid or lost
I'd like to read it again today
a lot has changed
during that long period.

Sometimes through a hole in the fence
I entered the town
the way there went by the gardens
across a flower bed a woman stretched out her body
in a swimsuit but not over-revealing
I'm not even sure if she was beautiful
her stomach nice and rounded
over her slightly parted thighs
almost made me fall over
With the dizziness
my eyes went blank
Just below in a small garden
you'd often see lying about
a kind of dishevelled
Brigitte Bardot
we got used to seeing each other like that
in a café in the square
where I go for a coffee that time of day
I once turn round
she is standing behind me
smiling at me in such a way
that I have to address her
but I'm not saying anything
and I'm getting out of here
and she gives me a gesture
that says I'm an idiot
And our love was over

All
I'd have longed for
and not only with her
was not to have to speak
meet her with a touch, be inside her
but such luck I've probably
never in my life deserved
or women gifted with
such sheer lasciviousness
don't inhabit this world
Then once during his rounds
Dr Kroulík
turns to me
this is no way to do things oh no
walking round town like a healthy person
citizens are complaining
that you might infect
the whole of Zamberk
I enjoyed the morning
but even more the afternoon
rest on the terrace
You could see into the park
in front of my deckchair two high larches
on one of them
a strangely twisted twig
would catch my eye
and below the park
all this would remind me
of some forgotten place and event
on a jaunt with my parents long ago
how we entered a garden restaurant
where after long wandering in summer heat
a kind shade received us
on the table a white tablecloth
cool granadine

Later on
Mr Franc got up very little
finally he stayed in bed the whole time
his father would come to see him
a little old man
I wouldn't have thought
he was a butcher too
he was suffering from TB
in the pavilion next door
he'd come and sit by the bed
tell me son how are you feeling better already
then he'd place his walking-stick
between his knees
rest his chin on it
and stay silent
both silent
we'd fall silent too general silence
Once Jirka came to see me
he brought the Skvoreck's with him
all of them had just become
stars in a film of the new wave
The Report of the Feast and the Guests
Jan Zabrana came with them too
I don't know what we talked about
I no longer remember
Once Ivan Pelc came to see me
On behalf of the editors
Honza Nedved would send me news
it was when the Central Committee of Writers
was deciding to dissolve Tvar
Helena Wernischova would write
letters to me with pictures
what good letters she wrote
which immediately after reading them
you responded to filled with hope

and the next letter threw cold water
In the next letter again
two or three silken words
Alena had saved a fortnight of her holiday
she had come with Jitka
and rented an apartment in Zamberk
we went on one happy trip together
to Kamenicna
Towards evening on the way back
it was already misty autumn
in an old general stores
a gas lamp was burning
All of a sudden we found ourselves
in an idyllic century
Apart from a very few
bright moments
we were tormenting each other
with endless accusations
My mum came every Sunday morning
I'd wait for her always by the gate
watching for her figure in the distance
She would leave towards evening
She'd bring a bag full of
carefully prepared dishes
that she thought I liked
Each time we spent the whole of Sunday
walking around the district
A cock crowed
It reminded her of home

Towards the autumn I met Vera
wife of a local doctor
at the end of our first walk together
during our first fleeting kiss
she felt me hard with her hand

she agreed to another walk next day
and in return she graciously
invited me to spend a gracious
afternoon with her family
I wrote to Hanka every day
and twice a week phoned her in Prague
always at about 2 p.m.
And I imagined jealously
what was going on in Prague
when Hanka is under the sole surveillance
of her own husband
Mr Franc was taken to the clinic
Someone brought the news
that he was lying in a plaster crust
his bones breaking already
soon after
came the death notice
That garden restaurant
was at the very back
of a large park
people were sitting at small tables
and the place
was neither crowded nor empty
on the right side
on the way from the park to the restaurant
I become aware of a tall silver spruce or fir
a silver fir I think
dad pointed it out to me
and here and there mighty deciduous trees
beeches perhaps

Prague 5 and 6 May 1987

Some Evening

Some evening we'll all sit down together
around thirty bottles,
me, you and Bob,
the two of you and me, the two of us and him,
someone is missing, but we'll only notice it
when we're already blind drunk,
sure, someone is missing here,
but I'm here, the missing one will say,
the one who is always with us,
the one always missing amongst us,
and on and on like that,
when we're completely drunk…

*

That night dawn is already breaking at 3a.m. on your
                          naked body,
Jarmila was asleep, I could hear her breathing
within reach of my hand, I'd have liked to stroke her
                          hair,
the whole night I was fearing
that she'd wake up…
So again it came to nothing, alas! that dream
to have them both together: two is the dream. Me lying
in the middle, Jarmila asleep, me afraid
she'd wake up. Let her sleep… she's blind drunk.
It's a trick, what is sleeping to my right
is my bled-to-death pain, I am aware
of every murmur of its breath, but
I am turning to your stomach.
We're moving slowly in a smaller space
than the smallest cell: the meeting of bowels,
in the corridor a door slammed, water rumbling,
le jour se lève.
In my youth – later too – I wanted to write like Jiri

41

Kolár.
And what came of it?
Waste of words.
It's night again
and I'm playing endlessly
over and over the same record
as that night when we didn't get round to turning the
player off
and during intercourse I was tempted
to match my movements to the music's rhythm
(I felt something funny was going on),
you kept gently restraining me
(the dance not right for the gravity of the moment),
but that light slowing down by you of the rhythm
was creating marvellous syncopes,
so marvellous I had to stop it
because I'd have had to start
laughing from sheer joy.

Don't you find, Alice,
that what I write is not written in poems?
(But is this really a poem?
Isn't it though, isn't it? I say,
self-destructive and unsure?)
For example Vladimir's pyjamas
and its buttoning system,
I couldn't undo it?
When my battle with the buttons
had exhausted my patience,
your fingers solved the problem
with a practised marital gesture
in a split second.

*

Where are the days
when I used to write beautiful verse!
I regret them desperately. But they are gone.
They are gone, departed,
and I am left stuck here.
All of a sudden I am old and surprised
it happened so unexpectedly.
                              *

I had a dream
that I'm sitting in the garden.
I hadn't been there in my dreams for a long time.
I was looking down towards the road,
in a small oval hole before me was a fireplace,
another one, round, behind my back,
I am realizing
that my uncle always tidied the garden
at this time in the autumn,
and when we are here
he never leaves the house.
From the hearths a little smoke was rising still.

                                        1974 to 1982

43

Pour S.

So you see it's day again, you see: by good fortune
we've weathered yet another night.
It was a miserable night,
as nights are in hospital.

And now I'm already home. Before
after being ill I used to feel triumphant,
as if I'd been born again;
I no longer have that feeling; there is darkness
where I am going, as if I'm propelled ahead.

Yesterday late at night we got back from Nikolaj's.
My mother woke up: she said I've had a bad dream.
I was dead, you were taking me somewhere,
somewhere, to a crematorium maybe,
I was dead and I knew everything.
Those dreams! Yesterday I dreamt how Daddy
(me: Daddy or Grandpa?)
grandpa, how he was dying. I gave him two spoons of
                                                    soup,
he didn't want any more. And I so desperate: Daddy,
please, eat.
It is bitterly cold, a clear icy January day,
just one more thing to say,
to preserve some of the memory of them all
whom I loved and was so useless to.
It doesn't go into words. Along with me
everything will go. Nothing will be left.
And what for? But I am only alive through
what was. What was is not. My dear, you
at least are alive while you live.

Sometimes at night I wake up in terror
and bend over my children
listening whether they are breathing.

And still we feel happy, sometimes.
And sometimes I'm amazed I can still be agitated,
when I see
the afternoon light reflected
in the glass of the westward windows.

I remember
what a relief it was
when once in the hospital, harassed,
gaunt, I caught a glimpse in the mirror —
somewhere in the X-Ray dressing-room —
my face.
Gaunt I looked like Pa
and I expressed my grief for myself by weeping.
The relief, that I can love myself.

What was beautiful and good
did not come of me
and I can't keep it alive within me.
And though I am touching it only lightly,
it is dying all the same.
But the bad things done,
they emerge sharply from the past.
They are unchallengably real
and present
like death.

1987

In Horní Ves

There were two suns
towards evening then.
'I dreamt', she said,
'that I am standing in the doorway
and my Mum
is calling me out to the garden,
that there are two suns in the sky.
And I tell her
how strange it is,
that I have already dreamt,
that we are standing together
on the very spot
and above the horizon
two suns as if through a filter
are showing through.'
And we were standing there,
living, real,
then, towards evening,
when above Vrch
two matt autumn
suns were setting.

And once at night
someone was banging on the gate.
I go to open it
and at the gate
my Mum – dead for thirty years.
The meeting made me happy,
But: 'How on earth, mum,
can you know
what family I married into?
And do you know that J. has died?'
'My little girl, I know everything...'

But at that point
I woke up
because someone had banged
on the gate.
But I didn't go
to open it.

It was at night again.
I walked out of the house
My dead sister,
white, was standing in the yard.
'What are you doing here?' I say.
And she: 'Today
J. is guarding the graveyard…'
And suddenly I see
how perhaps human flesh from the mouth…
God knows
what was going on there…

Along the road from Počátky
I was going home.
I knew
that everyone had died long before,
and yet, what joy!—
The lights were on at home.
I started running
like a madman.
At the kitchen table
my Dad was sitting,
but he was
looking at me reproachfully.

On the road to Cerekev
by the pond
there used to be – still is –
a forge.
Me and my Dad
used to pass by.
That year
we passed there
for the last time.
Then the pond was cut in two
by a new road.
In front of the forge
horses were shod.
Often we would stand there
for a long time.
Last summer
I went that way again.
The road had somehow grown stony
and overgrown.
And the stones on it
had turned black.
A dry stick
crackled under my foot.
Oh God! I am not writing poems,
I am crying.

My Dear Mourners

My dear mourners,
said the deceased,
My dear mourners —
he addressed them like that.
The only thing that is left now
is to pile up the earth over me
and to pile on me
the very best.
I am speaking
to relieve you of
that awkward duty
of telling the most innocent lies.
My dear mourners,
we are going to bury
our most innocent lie.
There,
where I am bound for,
is the eternal kingdom of worms,
but I
am already half-consumed.
The process began so long ago
that it's impossible to remember.
There,
where I am bound for,
is the kingdom of waters
and soil;
only now will begin
the birth of soil
from me.
And likewise
through the agency of rain
the loud-mouthed grave
will relieve itself of me.

As if it were quietly gargling…
No one will hear it,
it happens in silence.
That's the way it goes
in good families.
And we will remain
the most silent family,
and therefore at peace with worms.
My dear mourners,
do weep,
weep over the murmur
of my homily that will be echoed
by some nearby tree.
I am with it,
not with you;
neither did I lead a good life
nor did you all
love me.
My dear mourners,
there is no redemption.
The only hope is to rot,
and that began so long ago
it's hard to remember it.
Therefore rot,
my dear mourners,
so that there's at least something
you've got to the end of.

Mists

Someone heard a summons to court.
The weaklings snooped round the aspens
to find what truth was in it.
The leaves did not keep silence.

So the word got around.
In adolescent beds it was like
plucking up courage to snuff out a candle:
no one wanted to burn their finger
and there was no breath.

So this brief period
kept itself going like darkness.
Where the dark is bound
nobody knew.

And the first charge was heard:
that someone had coughed
us into the world already drunk
so there's no reason to be afraid
since we acted unbeknownst,
we the aborted foetus,
we already pronounced dead
by someone holding something back.

So stickily can mist too be generated,
the mist that rises from beds,
or from fine veins on the face
or from the breath of dead birds

rising from the depths of valleys.
Such is the mist
from the mating of mammals,
the mist too
concealed in dreams,
such the mist
in the bloodshot eyes of predators,
the mist in moss.

Along the Paths

Along the beast-trodden paths
from grass a bog builds up.
Small birds' feathers in the shrubs
drooping. Rain, rain, rain.

It froze at night. So in the morning
the flash of fens will shine.
Silence. From the village a bell toll
and a wail.

Little Deaths

Little deaths
dwell in birds' light corpses.
With the echo of their wings
they beat against our cheeks.
In the end green water
rains down on all.
A dog quietly slinks
in by the door…

Snow

Snow.
Animals shrunk to the bone,
small mouths torn by thorn-trees,
so a white time,
as if angels
(once maybe aflame?)
have burnt to ashes.

All colour burned from the landscape.
Tears quenched in eyes of ice.
Ailing small bodies of children,
shroudlets of white mist.

When it is Raining

When it is raining,
the pond
as if just convalescing
from smallpox.
Below under the dam
the chub are gorging on the rain.
Afterwards
the moon reveals itself to girls,
pressing its attentions on
the chaste straw.
And in the little knuckles
how tenderly the straw crackles!
But beneath the dam
appear
the white bodies
of drowned women.

I Was Walking

I was walking
by the abattoir.
At that time
it was only there
the small gate opened.
Through a dormer window you could see
a rope hanging
at all times.
As far as the eye could see,
a tree nowhere around
was alive.
Far away
a train was whistling.
In the gate's masonry the stone
overgrown by sour moss.
An old woman in the yard, on her knees,
a bird's throat was dying.

Variations on Gelner III
To Sergej

The waters will stay, the woods will stay,
cities inhabited by new populace.
Someone will be hanged, someone else won't
and life will go merrily on.

The traces of murder will be blown away
from this century's sand.
Mute victims with their executioners
will still loom here in an icy embrace.

(Gelner was a decadent poet who died very young in World War I.
Sergej was a friend of Hejda's who used to be pro-communist but
became disillusioned. S.D.)

I was Supposed to Cross a Bridge

I was supposed to cross a bridge. It was an iron bridge, narrow for a single person and long, very long. Under the bridge the river was stationary, but it was not important that it was not flowing, nor did it matter that it was dark. The thing was that I had stopped in the middle of the bridge. Not stopped exactly but I was in the middle of the bridge with already half of the journey behind me, but I had no memory of that journey: I only knew I had half the bridge behind me. Now I am sitting here and I know I have to go on to the end but I am not moving. It is clear to me I must stand up and go on, but I'm not doing it; though I am not aware of any obstacle or danger, I am not proceeding. I am slowly slipping down, my legs are dragging, and if I don't stand up and go on I will slide down into the water; but that doesn't bother me. And again: I know I have to get to the end... And I just keep sitting there.

Daring Arches Over the Eyes

Daring arches over the eyes,
marvellous red boats of lips…
The winter will come, the winter will pass…
and ice will sweep away the bridge…

Chinese Poets

Chinese poets,
those old Chinese poets,
they get drunk and peer heavenwards
where migrating geese tow
in their trail the sadness of autumn.
Or they gaze at
the water's surface
at their own reflections
and paint verses
about a plum twig in bloom.

Oh! These old
Chinese poets who
distil from drunkenness the poetry of age.

A Poem whose Beginning got lost

...what to add?
Excusez, monsieur, it was
in the year 69 on the way from England
in a street running down from Montmartre,
somewhere round there
she ran out of a house
dressed hurriedly,
a coat slipped over her shoulders,
and when she bumped into me softly,
excusez monsieur...
I'd have liked to live there –
somewhere round there.
Somewhere round there
just at the same time
S. was living
in rue Germain Pilon.
Then we couldn't
meet yet.
Mr Reynek wrote to me:
'The little butterfly of luck is always
on the far side of the glass',
and enclosed a picture
of a window with a butterfly
on the far side of the glass.

I'm walking along Štěpánská street and I'm so damn
lucky

I run into Magor,
swaying a bit:
put it this way – swaying a lot,
astonished by the news
that Chinese poets
would write their verses

in a state of drunkenness:
totally legless from rice liqueur.
And I said:
have you noticed that Chinese poets
are all old men?
Thus we exchanged
valuable knowledge
about Chinese poets.
All my life I have
rather longed for Japanese women.
And – why not admit it? –
also:
to watch
the garden from the window
of the cool shaded semi-darkness of a stone house in
summer,
from the kitchen
where the clock is ticking loudly,
to watch trembling leaves, branches,
the shadow-fall
on to the whitewashed wall
drawn by the shade.

(S. is the poet's wife Susette.Šimon Daníček)

Where on earth

Where on earth
have I wandered into
as if into some
joyful painting?
Frightened, I've at once
turned back.